TRIUMPH HOUSE
Poetry with a Purpose

CASTAWAY DREAMS

Edited by

Steve Twelvetree

First published in Great Britain in 2001 by
TRIUMPH HOUSE
Remus House,
Coltsfoot Drive,
Peterborough, PE2 9JX
Telephone (01733) 898102

HB ISBN 1 86161 900 6
SB ISBN 1 86161 905 7

FOREWORD

In this busy and hectic world in which we live, it is easy to take for granted the little things that make and mould our lives. In this unique anthology the authors try to imagine what life would be like all alone on a deserted island.

Over 100 poets have combined their talents to bring to you a delightful selection of poetry on a subject that is sure to be discussed time and time again.

How would you react, and what would your first thoughts be? The poems range dramatically in both style and content from cries for help, to messages to loved ones.

So sit back and take in all this wonderful anthology has to offer.

Steve Twelvetree
Editor

CONTENTS

SOS

I have always wanted an island of dreams
But suddenly now, it's not what it seems
I am at that moment, the moment of truth.
There is no one around, it's the quietest sound.
Sounds of silence, sounds of fear
Sounds of knowing there is no one here.
Sounds of the sea, as it splashes
It's like my mind as it flashes
SOS - Stranger on the shore.

So I put my message in this bottle, hoping it will be found
Not so far from where I have run aground.
But in case this is my final message, I will try not to sound sad
Because truthfully, life hasn't really been that bad.
I have sailed south on these seas, only to be washed upon this shore
Timeless moments make me realise, there is so, so much more.
So to the finder of my message in this bottle
Help me if you can, if you are too late, then please let it be understood
Life is to be lived, love is to be shared, Health is a bonus,
So, make your life good.

Pauline Porteous

CHANGE OF ADDRESS

Should this bottle stay afloat
And someone find this note
And helps to send it on its rightful way
It's to tell you I am stranded -
On an island I have landed
And I am queen of all that I survey.

As I've nothing much to do here
I thought I'd write to *you* dear,
And the reason's very simple, I'll explain:
If this note survives the deep
I shall not lose any sleep
Waiting for an answer, that's quite plain.

I shall not survey the skies,
Nor scan the sea with anxious eyes,
Neither keep a beacon burning through the night.
I shall rest beneath the palm trees,
Enjoy the sunshine and the sea breeze,
Because I know that *you* will never write.

So I can use my sense of fun
In requesting you, dear son,
To send to me by ship, or plane, or rocket:
A little house that's ready made
To afford much needed shade;
A microwave, complete with plug and socket.

A table, chair, and comfy bed
Or, if you like, instead -
A show house, filled with contents, to possess,
And you can send me grocery orders
Every week across the borders
Of all the food I like from M & S.

If this note should ever find you,
It may serve to remind you
You've not written for about a year, I guess.
But at one time or another
You will remember me, your mother,
So please note that now I have a new address.

Shirley H Ford

Bottle On The Beach

To you who read this, from one isolate
in midst of ocean, in a here and now
which indicates an end of mortal state
unless some rescue Providence allow;

Our hands now touch across how many years?
Your present moment interlaced with mine;
our fundamental human hopes and fears
in common held within one great design.

If, when you read this, I be dead and gone,
it is no matter; time itself, and space,
are timeless, spaceless. One, the light that shone
on me and shines on you; one fond embrace

by message in a bottle, more or less,
to greet you and, if you allow it, bless!

Anthony Duncan

MESSAGE IN A BOTTLE

It's strange to be writing like this
But these days I feel rather scared:
As, watching the ebbing of tides,
Of life I begin to despair.
So I'm anxious to let you know
I'm intact and safe enough here,
Somehow I've ridden the tide to
The rock of my forty-ninth year.
It's strange how I just bobbed along
Unsure how I got to this place,
My landmarks all seem to have gone,
The route I shall never retrace.
Yet inside I feel just the same
(I hope that I make myself clear)
Now something has got to be done:
I'm certain I don't like it here.
I have checked out my position,
Making time to take a good rest,
Before slipping back into the
Water, returning to my quest.
Leaving my rock in the distance,
Swimming strongly on out to sea,
I'll reach for gold in the sunset -
So please keep a look out for me.

Patrick B Osada

Island In The Sun

Stranded on the desolate beach
I stand and watch the sea
And dream of the life I once had
And how I wished to be free.

And now I'm here on this island
Washed ashore with the remains of the ship,
With a cocktail in my hand
I took my one last sip.

Now alone to sit and ponder
With my memories carried along on a breeze,
I built a place called home
In the shade of coconut trees.

And wondered how I lived my life
On days that just seemed nice
And had a vision such as this,
This place called Paradise.

Debbie Twine

Shopping List

Whoever finds this letter in the glass,
A bottle that once held a lovely wine,
I hope that you will be a man of class
Who's willing to supply these needs of mine.

I do not wish to leave this precious isle,
Nor yet to live here in this solitude,
But with your help once more I'll live in style
With comfort, happiness and well-cooked food.

So please, kind finder of this precious note,
I ask that you will not this stranger fail;
Put all the things I ask for in a boat
And to this lovely island quickly sail.

I need a fishing rod to catch my meal
And a hammer to split all the coconuts,
A box of books, and ought else you can steal,
And to catch the rain a pair of water butts.

Bring all of these, and there is one thing more
For I must have a lovely lady fair;
Find one and bring her to my shore,
And then I think I'll need a rocking chair.

Then with these things I'll have all I will need
To live a life of ease just as I wish;
With rod I'll fish, then eat, then rest and read,
And there will be the girl to cook the fish.

The Wandering Bard

Shipwreck

An island trapped me in its hot embrace,
the very symbol of an ancient race,
its ruins from a time when man was king,
tore at my soul and made my senses sing.
Then, dawn came and I knew the score,
of water there would be no more.
So now I'm writing a note just for you
my God I hope you pull me through.
Remember your old branch and bough,
the fruit I bore well, it has ripened now,
it just needs you to let it take a bow,
it still may need my council in a row.
Throwing this bottle far out from the shore,
I hope you help me like you did before.

Jean Paisley

SERENDIPITY ISLAND

To the finder of this message,
Please don't rescue me,
I'm writing, just to let you know,
I'm happy as can be.

I've been here for a while now,
In fact, I'm quite at home,
I'm on this desert island,
So peaceful here, alone.

There are no noisy neighbours,
No motorbikes or cars,
No jet planes over,
Just me, beneath the stars.

I have no need of money,
No plastic cards or cheques,
No bills come through my letterbox,
In fact, I've got no debts.

There are no politicians,
No Presidents or Kings
No red tape, or officials,
To argue over things.

There is no drug addiction,
No people without hope,
No crisis in the hospitals,
With nurses that can't cope.

You could say, I'm in paradise,
My serendipity,
So I will say it once again,
Please don't rescue me.

Jim Sargant

LETTER IN A BOTTLE

Captain Ted, on an island, surrounded by sand
  kept watching horizons in case help was on hand,
a glint in the water catches his weary eye
  he saw a corked bottle and he let out a cry.

He opened the bottle, washed up on the beach,
  inside was a paper in too far to reach
so he smashed the old bottle and pulled out a note
  and fished for his specs from inside his coat.

'Please help. I'm marooned after sinking my ship
  somewhere on the ocean three days in the trip,
I'm south of the line that runs round the earth
  and east of the one that gives new days a birth.'

'I'm hot and I'm hungry and very afraid
  and waiting for someone to come to my aid.
The fishes are friendly and help me to thrive
  and a fresh-water stream to keep me alive.'

Ted studied the writing, the date and the name
  and noticed with horror his was one of the same,
this letter was one he had posted last year
  now someone had added a devilish jeer.

'I regret very much I signed for that trip
  I'm marooned same as you and from the same ship,
if you hadn't got drunk we'd still be afloat
  and you wouldn't have run into that larger steamboat.

Our boat, overloaded, just sank like a stone
  and into the sea the crew were all thrown,
and if by some chance I survive this abyss
  I promise you Captain, I'll give you a miss.'

Leslie Holgate

Rescue Me

The sea's as blue as azure, the sand as white as snow.
The grass as green as any that in England's soil does grow.
The palm trees must stand close to fifty metres high
With leaves that form a canopy that hides from me the sky.
The rivers flow like silver with water pure and clean
And in them swim the largest fish that I have ever seen.
This desert isle's as perfect as it could ever be,
Yet I've thrown a bottle with this message into the sea.
It's a very simple message. Will someone rescue me?

There is no one here to talk to, no one to share this wonderland.
No one here to go on walks with, strolling hand in hand.
No one to share a joke with or to tell a story to.
No one to eat a meal with as once I used to do.
No one to laugh or cry with, I'm left here quite alone.
And I can't stand the isolation of being all on my own.
For me to go on living I must have some company.
And so in desperation I wrote out my heartfelt plea.
I can't tell you where I'm stranded but come and rescue me.

It can only be about a fortnight that I've been in this place
But I've become desperate to see another human face,
It's certainly true that man can bring trouble, grief and woe
And that he can pollute the earth wherever he does go.
But I have come to realise that however beautiful this land
It's man that makes life worth living. I hope you understand.
So when you read my message, wherever you may be,
Know that you're hearing from a man who's feeling very lonely
And please do everything you can to come and rescue me.

M J Scutter

IT'S ALL PRETEND

As I look into the mirror and see
what's inside,
I wonder what secrets the girl in
there has to hide,
The face I see smiles but I do not,
It doesn't really look like me a lot.
The eyes are more friendly,
The smile more wide,
With the face of someone with a
warm face inside.
But the girl in the mirror is just
a guard,
Of a person who is lonely,
cold and hard,
The reflection moves and
fades away,
And the mirror is left empty,
cold and grey.

Harriet Forkin (12)

Cast Adrift

'Abandon Ship!' Captain yells
Through gangways, cold water swells.
Chaos everywhere, there're terrified screams
Suddenly comes ocean's cruel reams
Helplessly thrashing towards upturned boat
Desperately trying to keep afloat
Exhaustion, overtakes them I've found
Myself delivered upon firm ground
Completely alone, days became endless
Cast adrift, so totally friendless
Eating clams, drinking murky waters
Thinking of son, my two baby daughters
My husband, my babies. Are they alive?
Oh dear God, did my family survive?
Without proper food, death came calling
As into abyss, I felt myself falling
Knowing death was near at hand
Reaching towards only possessions on the sand
There lay my only hope, Pepsi Cola.
Paper, pen and a solid water folder
Writing SOS - someone hear my plea
Save my life, please set me free.
Setting bottle down on surfy waves
As Soul prepared for fathoms graves
Days passed, when giving up all hope
There on horizon, sailed a boat
Blurry images ran over beach
When at last my ebbing body they reach
My husband's voice came sweet and clear
'You're safe at last, my darling dear.'

Ann Hathaway

An Island I Am Not

I'm an island on an island
Wrapped around by sea.
Deliver me from drowning here
Cut off from company!

At first I chose this way of life
To fly away alone
Embraced the quiet, left the strife
No house, or telephone.

I wanted to be by myself,
To take a peaceful stance,
And sit down in a hermit's seat
Or wander in a trance.

This lovely island did at first
Yield its treasures galore.
I found such beauty in its face.
Its body yielded more.

It's shown me a deep secret
I'll carry in my heart.
We all need some silence
But we never are apart.

I need the equilibrium,
The fellowship of those
Who follow in the footsteps of
Life's poetry and prose.

Please! Rescue me and take me back!
This hope is all I've got.
Join me to mainland again,
An island I am not.

Judith Thomas

OPEN ALL HOURS

Take this offering
a simple gift of words
that transcends the tools I have

my doors are open to you
but you are already here
I whisper and you hear me
arms around me like the ocean
I am at your mercy.

Benjamin F Jones

ISLAND OF REFLECTION

(Date possibly mid August 2001)

To the recipient of this note, (I hope that you can read English)
cast adrift in the bottle which I held on to, now minus its amber nectar,
it may seem a little pointless to you,
that I am about to recap on those misspent days of youth.
Once they stretched before me, seemingly endless as I scanned
the horizon.
So many things taken for granted, opportunities missed,
believing that there was always tomorrow.
Working long hours with no time for myself, I had tried to fill
every hour,
since early retirement was thrust on by redundancy.
I wished to attain yesterday's dreams, before taking the final journey,
like throwing a pot or two *(and not just in the kitchen).*
I now realise that I stand on that distant horizon, up the creek
without a paddle.

I should have known not to take the cruise offered at cut price,
complete with a pair of oars and a do-it-yourself manual.
So here I am on a sun-kissed idyllic island, without lipstick and
toilet paper.
I really do miss the luxury of a bathroom, a comfy sofa and TV.
Golden sand it has to be said, cannot compare to a double bed
and duvet.
Of late, that is before being stranded,
(With just a coconut palm for company, incidentally virtually barren),
in my quest for knowledge, many books have passed through my hands,
wherein the bones of our ancestors reveal, man and his origins.
At some future point will mine be discovered buried upon this beach,
dusted and catalogued, browsed over and discussed.
The indigo night sky is a glorious sight where silver stars glide
in motion.

I now contemplate all that the one Creator set into motion,
whilst craving for a plate of chips, plus roast chicken and jacket potato.
As the days here blend into each other,
it is a stark reminder of the material world with its ticking clock,
I have time to reflect on my place in the system,
realising that I am a speck in the ocean about me *(a frightening thought).*

The chances of being rescued seem a million to one.
The local inhabitants, (apes) occasionally throw down a banana,
unfortunately for me I have always been allergic to them,
and as there is no doctor in the house, *(I mean island)* I am not tempted.
(I can hear a sound), help! Send help! Help! I am not alone, it's a . . .
(Oh no! The pencil lead is brea . . . k . . . i . . .

Ann G Wallace

LOVE'S RETURN

A perfect sky
when love came through -
It's depth no earthly words
define -

Travelled love cross miles
of tempestuous sea
Life's meaning shared
of a love sublime.

Where e'er you walk
and those you love
Whom I too love with
unspoken bliss -
My love enfolds in
mystic cloud
and travels back with
true love's kiss.

Here on this isle - your
love unfolds
From bottled memories
in Rich Design -
Through oceans deep I
cross my heart
To declare a love
Forever Thine.

Mary Skelton

The Message In The Bottle

You're there in the glass bottle of your
life, and you're making money and
you're living, aren't you? Heading for the
high life - the champagne years,
a heady cocktail, life and love . . . Only,
the walls of the bottle, they're opaque,
after all, and you don't see:
no, you don't see life and you don't
see love at all: and you're
only a message in a bottle, that's all.

And then you're here: a desert island, and
there's nothing but sand, sky - and you
and your soul. And there's just one set
of footprints: and the sun, beating down:
and at night the moon, and the stars.

And there's all this light, linking,
linking everything: you in the silence
of your soul, quietening, and the world
that hurries on beyond an unseen horizon.

And through the glass walls of your heart,
there's something you see: something in you,
linking you with the light - with all around you.
And deep and moist in the sand
there're two sets of footsteps, walking side
by side, walking a long pathway to
the sun and stretching on, beyond the
horizon. And the walls of your heart
clear - and you see, you see - you're
so much more than a message in
a bottle, after all . . .

Jocelyn McKinnon

THE ONLY WAY

Is there anyone in space
Who could teach us how to live?
We have a lovely planet
But we've only learned to fight, not to forgive.
You'd think we'd be so grateful
That we'd love it and enjoy it,
But, actually, we do our worst
To pollute it and destroy it,
And we kill our fellow creatures
In stupid senseless wars
And cherish all our 'victories'
And demand the crowd's applause.

Well, years went by and no reply
Had ever been received;
And those who thought 'There's no one there'
Said 'Now we'll be believed!'

But then, at last, a message came
How it survived - who knows?
They thought they'd have to crack the code;
Perhaps the papers would explode?
But, no, it was secure.
They took it to their President
Who opened it and said -
'My friends, this has been Heaven sent;
It says you've gathered all the crops
That in your greedy past you've sown,
So I'll remind you of my Son -
Just go the Way that He has shown;
The way to live has long been known.'

Leo Taylor

WISHING YOU WERE HERE

There's a silver, full moon pathway
Right across the sea tonight.
There's a cushioned, velvet canopy
With trillion stars of light
High above me
And I wish that you were here

There's a zephyr breeze just starring
In the trees within the park
There's an almost holy silence
Which gathers in the dark
And I feel the peace
And wish that you were here

There's a gentle yap-yap-yapping
Of some dogs out for a walk
And the sound of human voices
As their owners stroll and talk
And I say a prayer
And wish that you were here.

There are oh! so many memories
In my mind and in my heart
There were things we did and words we spoke
Before we had to part
And I almost feel
That you are really here.

Catherine May

Poisoned Bottle

Floating around in the poisoned sea,
this is a message from me, to you.
Please don't put me in the sea again,
it's full of effluence, from mankind's drains.
Stand me on a shelf, pop in a candle,
display my shiny, textured glass.
But please don't leave me floating around,
with the stools of mankind's arse.

Among the poisons of mankind's waste,
an untainted, pristine bottle,
repulsed by the taste.

Danny Coleman

Shipwrecked Sand

Dearest Julie, sand
time trickled sand
flesh warming sand
beating heat
stumbling feet
I love you
my love
sand
sad stretching sand
tree-lined sand
burning hide
turning tide
I hear voices
spoiling choices
sand
soft surrounding sand
wet-windblown sand
boiling skin
suffered sin
ocean reflecting blue
visions of you
sand
red remorseless sand
ever endless sand
throbbing sun
loaded gun
my time is near
goodbye my dear
forever, John 'Jolly' Johnson
out of Whitby

Chris Bailey

Missing You

Who would have thought that wishes come true
I really wanted to get away from all of you
So here I am, all alone
Thinking of you all back home

I'm surrounded by sand and sea
But there's no one here to talk to me
The sun is hot, the sky so blue
But oh how I miss all of you

Husband you were always so busy
Children your demands drove me dizzy
And so I wished for a quiet retreat
Now all I have is heat, heat, heat

I miss your laughter and your tears
How long will I be here? How many years
A little peace we all sometimes need
But before you wish for it, please take heed

Sandra Marie Laird

Clawed Law

volcano of moist sand
bubbling watered grain
erupts
harsh light of day
black pincered claw
emerges
followed staring stalks
hauling armoured body
effortlessly
safety of darkened den
crystallised silicon grounds
encrusting
glistening reflective wet
illuminating sloping shell
external
hardened hat crawling
sideways shuffled stride
edging

Luke Thomas

Good For Her!

I don't know why our common comrades
insist on updating me
with your current status -
each misfortune,
every titbit of happy news.

They must know - it had oft been displayed
for any and all to see -
my love is a lattice,
a vast compound
of emotions founded around you.

It must show *(must)* that I am dismayed
by your absence, never free
of memories; that is
never immune
to each torment you endure, each bruise,

each joy. Yet that litany's replayed
over and over . . . frailly -
wait of phrase once fat as
a pig - dry tune
of 'Good for her!' shredding soul anew.

Perry McDaid

A Message In A Bottle

The rain falls warm - gentle on my upturned palm
I anoint my skin with the scented oils
It is almost a healing balm
To the wound that my leg bears to this very day.
I want you to know I have been happy here.
The island has become Shangri La to me.
All the tiny creatures have become my willing friends
I collect flotsam from the shore.
The fish are in great abundance too.
I wear the frangipani in my hair
And pray you were saved from the ship.
The fragrances of sandalwood are all about me!
I have swam many times in the blue lagoon
And found a treasure of pearls that I bequeath to you
There is a cave where I rest at nights
It is sheltered by the palm.
The turtle comes at Eventide
He has become my night-time friend!
The sea horses gave a beautiful display last night
I am placing a kiss for you within the bottle green.
A tall dark stranger with a beard
Walks towards me from the shore!
Not a footprint has he made!
He tells me all is well!
And lifts me with such gentleness!
And says 'Do not fret little one, your love will come and
find your treasure!

D Brook

A TRINITY

Have you seen how things are often in threes
Like Father and Mother with the baby you see;
Israel has Christian, Moslem and Jew
Where Mary, Joseph and Jesus lived too.
In Bosnia, Croats with Moslems and Serbs;
But your kitchen may have only three herbs.
You have at your table, knife, fork and spoon
And get light from the sun, the stars and the moon.
Rain, sleet and snow are three others we know
While buses and trains can stop, start or go.
Red, amber and green in the high street are seen,
When traffic lights change, you know what it means
And so it goes on, never ending you see,
But the last three will be without doubt,
RIP.

Stan M Tweedie

A MAN FOR ALL SEASONS

I'm writing this message my only plea
For someone to come and rescue me.
My ship was wrecked, I'm all alone
On this sandy island as dry as bone.
Until this moment I've always dreamt
Of heavenly silence and wild flower scent,
Deep blue sea and swaying palms
Passionate nights in my lover's arms.
But this is different he is not here
I'm oh so lonely and low in cheer,
I cannot survive without my man
So find him and send him if you can.
And if you do you can ignore
My plea for rescue and that's for sure,
But maybe a few more hunky men
Will make life worth living once again.

Joan Twine

TRAIN OF THOUGHT

My eyes slowly open
There is a shape in the haze
Just an island
Sitting there in the sea
Not a boat, not a footprint
There is something that says
Just the ocean, this island and me.

So peaceful and quiet
There is hardly a sound
Just the sea
Licking sand from the beach
Not a gull, not a cloud
There is nothing around
Just palm trees with fruit out of reach.

Sun high in the sky
There is hardly a breeze
Just enough
To keep my face cool
Not a care, not a worry
There is no one to please
Just my shadow at my feet like a pool.

My eyes slowly open
There is a shape in the haze
Just a guard
Looking down as I lay
Not the peace, not the quiet
There is something that says
Just more Hell on this Burma railway.

Merv Pack

Message In A Bottle

It's the 23rd March 1935,
I've been left alone on the island,
I just feel alive
These are my last words, my final postcard.
I suppose I've lived a good life,
Full of love, happiness and joy.
I'll never forget the first time
I kissed a pretty girl, the feeling,
The touch, she had a spell on me.
To my mother, I send you my love,
You made me, shaped me, cared for me,
Without you I'm nothing.
Memories can never be bought.
To my brothers, I send warm wishes
But grief for your love.
To my friends, Dave and Frank,
What a great holiday we shared
In New York City, our friendships
Were real, funny and beautiful, honest.
Your humour was brilliant, crystal and bright.
So as the island light fades
And my heart feels grey
I end this note
I hope it gets home.

Andrew Ryan

FIFTH NOVEMBER FLOOD ZERZERO

Noise after the light
River roars by
I'm sat on a bank
With a two mile waterfall
Just behind me

The world is changing
This world is changing
Yeah, yeah, yeah
Our world is changing

The red half
Of the moon
Look so dry
Not a cloud in the sky
But tomorrow
Just have to wait
And see

The world is changing
This world is changing
Yeah, yeah, yeah
Our world is changing

The fireworks begin to fly
Like a broken rainbow
Flashing in the sky

The world is changing
This world is changing
Yeah, yeah, yeah
Our world is changing

SLL

HAIKU IN A BOTTLE

I long for rescue
Hot bath, roast beef and friendship
My hope's in your hands.

Brenda Dove

Lonesome Days

I thought that I would sail away to a foreign land,
But I am stranded now, with all around me sand,
My small boat made a funny sound and sunk amid some bubbles,
That's the reason I am here, the start of all my troubles.

All I have is what I wear, gone are all my treasures,
I hope this bottle will be found, I'm taking drastic measures,
I have not slept since I arrived, I walk around all night,
I wish I had a water bed to help me in my plight.

The sun is hot and I am ill with the tidal motion,
If this note is found, oh please, bring me suntan lotion,
As yet I have not seen a ship, I'm going mad I fear,
At times I think that in the sand I see a glass of beer.

When this bottle reaches land, don't delay, but hurry,
Bring me quickly vintage wine and a plate of curry,
I hope you find me very soon, so easing my distress,
I'm enclosing for your help, my present new address.

I have walked around for miles, nothing can I see,
Not a living soul in sight, not a single tree,
Dusky maidens I had hoped to greet me on the shore,
But alas, I am alone, and life is now a bore.

My trousers are now tattered, bring another pair,
Don't forget the scissors to cut my knee length hair,
I do not have a mirror, I feel I now look weird,
Today when I was walking I tripped up on my beard.

Tell the pals in my home town how I miss them sadly,
Ask if they would mow my lawn, it may need it badly,
I forgot to leave a note to cancel all my papers,
Ask my wife to walk the dog and don't get up to capers.

I will keep a lookout and hope you will come soon,
You will hear me calling and baying at the moon,
If you are delayed and perhaps arrive at night,
You will find my island second on the right.

A H Thomson

AH, MY TREASURE

Cannon balls of glass arched across my bow,
 the bow of the illusory Pimpernel.
This was my Armada, his merely the Rybow
 so how could he sound my death knell.

Alas, he seeks me here, he seeks me there
 but my smokescreen blinds his vision.
He discharges his armoury everywhere
 but fails to complete his mission.

Refuge, safety in the arms of my true love
 knowing in deep waters foes abide.
Indeed, piracy and deceit lurk above
 but within our smokescreen, we hide.

Lo, those that seek me, seek my treasure;
 of maps, chests and glimmering jewels they dream
yet they do not have our measure
 and we cause things to be not what they seem.

Adoration, yea, I adore this my treasure,
 my ship, my vessel of flesh and bone.
We are soulmates, in each other we have pleasure,
 sailing seas, yet apart, alone.

Someday my love, I may sail ashore
 away from the mighty storms at sea
to take our ease, be at one, to adore
 to love, to be together, you and me.

Lloyd Noyes

THIS HAND

This hand
once gave its thumb
into my soft sucking lips
to comfort the crying baby

This hand
once twiddled and fiddled
with needle and thread
to make pretty dresses for dolls

This hand
has held a million
crying faces
and dried the rivers of tears

This hand
now holds the reed
and tries to scratch out
this hopeful note

This hand
needs yours to hold
and feel my need
for ripening life

Please save this hand -
its life's work has only just begun . . .

Jane Phillimore

STRANDED

I am stranded on an island, we drifted out to sea,
there is no food, can not find no shelter for me,
there are no people here, it is such an empty place,
I am surviving on sea water, it has not a nice taste.
I need some food, I would like a juicy steak,
a slice of baked bread or even a cake,
I am sending this letter because there is nothing else I can do,
I picked a few berries but a fever they gave me too.
Say hello to my family and whoever finds this letter,
I hope it is not long now before I come home and get better,
I feel very weak as I look out on the empty sea,
I hope I see a ship soon wherever can they be.
I found some stones and sticks to make a fire,
I would rather be somewhere where I could have a car to hire.

Sally Warren

THE WORLD'S MOST WANTED MAN

This beautiful blonde on a desert island stands
Wriggling her ten tiny toenails in the sand
Waiting, hoping, trying to be brave
Praying that her dream man will soon cross the waves
With my great suntan as the soft breeze fans
And my soft sand-smoothed, outstretched hands
Because our big white ship has sunk in the bay
And the other silly girls and boys swam the other way
Only one leaning palm tree shelters poor little me
And I vowed to marry the first free man I see.

You're a millionaire, so what
I don't mind what you've got
So long as you arrive on a seaworthy yacht.
Hurry! I'm a writer - but I've almost lost the plot!
Yes. I'm the sort of girl who appreciates champagne
But if our eyes meet over ice cubes I will not complain
I've had baths in waves for days so bring a shower, not a bath
And a solitaire, a laptop and a great big laugh!

I must confess I'm dreaming of a shipping millionaire
But any millionaire would love me - what travel tales
we'll have to share!
A cruise ship owner, pilot, newsman, that would suit me too.
I'm only thinking, darling, of what I could do for you.
I'd be bored staying stuck on this island forever
Where the sky is my TV and its programmes are the weather.
I'd rather be in London than the tropical outdoors.
Bring a chopper, island-hopper or a yacht and I'm yours!

Turn this page to navigate the waves. My number's underneath.
E-mail the mobile in my pocket, love, and rocket to my reef.

Angela Lansbury

It Does Not Matter

Alone on this island staring out to sea,
It is so much easier for me
To tell you how I feel.
How I have let you steal
My heart,
Which has been torn apart.
How I see your face,
And my heart starts to race.
How I wish to look in your eyes,
And I pray you have no ties.
But I look away,
As I do not know what to say.
Maybe if I give you a smile,
But then I would run a mile.
Afraid to let you know
My feelings, to show
You my love.
If only we could fit together like a hand and glove.
But I am scared to discover,
In case you have another,
Or you do not feel the same.
In case you decide to play some sort of game,
With my heart and mind.
Maybe love is blind.
This message in a bottle may never get to you.
You will never know who
I am, but now there is no need to hide
My feelings, to keep them locked inside
My heart, as now it does not matter if you care
And it does not matter that I was there.

Elizabeth Jones

One Tiny Seashell

One tiny seashell lying in the sand
Is the only object for miles around;
On either side the coastline stretches,
Curving back behind me as the desert island
Blends with infinity behind ocean blue.

The sand's very softness is treacherous -
An eternity of yellow solitude
Unbroken by homeland's browns or greens;
My footprints the only sign of life
In a world of ochre and azure.

I bend down to pick up the shell. Half buried
In lonely desolation, it peeps out
From the sand; and as I hold it up
To bright sunlight it weeps salt tears -
Just a drop too many.

One tiny fan-shaped conch in whose depths
I hear the distant roar of happier seas,
And glimpse the smiles of friends long gone.
I look around for childhood sandcastles,
But gaze into empty nothingness.

One last desperate attempt. Leaving
My glass bottle in the sand beside my shell,
I follow the shoreline, combing in vain;
But in half an hour I'm back to my bottle,
And back to my first footprints.

My gnawing stomach tells me at last:
'There is only one thing more to be done'.
I uncork my bottle. The conch will just go in;
And I wrap around it my message of hope:
'Death is not the end. Jesus loves you.'

Robert D Hayward

MESSAGE FROM A BOTTLE

I am alone on my island of thought,
A castaway and exiled - cursed
To seek my origin in ideas fraught
With pregnant sin that waits to burst
And spurt and spill in gory thrill
On the church's inculcated will.

I am alone on my island of dreams
Awaiting my expurgation: -
Not seeking my salvation. For it seems
That's nothing less than annihilation
In the dregs of an empty bottle.
'What is left?' I merrily chortle!

I am alone on my island that's life.
I grasp the present in my grateful hand,
Not just existing but fully alive;
An integral part of this native land.
No longer a flotsamed refugee
Drifting lonely in an empty sea.

I am alone on the island I've claimed
As my own. I'm newly liberated
And have reached the zenith for which I aimed,
Free of the universally hated
Precepts. Master of my cerebral isle
I raise a wistful, knowing smile.

Mor Maciver

DON'T BOTTLE IT UP!

A message in a bottle - that's written from the heart,
A message that is blurring - please let it be the start,
A message in a bottle - of messy running ink,
A message in a bottle - from one who's at the brink,
A message that could surely dwindle - until it all has gone,
An outlook for a country - because people cannot get along,
A message that is burning - as it passes through the air,
A serious kind of message - that brings fear and great despair,
A message for another - who has become an enemy,
A message in a bottle - that says 'Stay away from me'
A message filled with heartache - for leaders won't agree,
A message that is empty - for those across the sea,
A bottle with a message - of hope for coming love,
A message that's endorsed - by he who dwells above,
A message stained and blemished - as bombers hear the thud,
A message they're ignoring - as innocents feel the blood,.
I have an urgent message - read it before it is gone,
It will not need the bottle - if we can get along,
A message in a bottle - let it be from He above,
Let this message be the ending - of war replaced with love.

John L Wright

HELP

Help, help won't you please help
I'm stuck on this island not even a piece of kelp.
It's dry and it's hot and it is lonely
I've no one to talk to
If you get my message
Please find me and call me
Help, help, help

Joseph Wilshaw (12)

LIFE IN A BOTTLE

When I came to,
I was lying on a beach,
Washed there by the tide and good fortune,
I remember that awful monsoon,
Which turned the ship to matchwood,
Then threw us to the waves,
And for most early watery graves.

I'm lucky to be alive, I'm thinking,
As I start to gain my senses,
A feeling of isolation dawns,
In earnest I walk along the beech,
Following my nose, my intuition,
Hoping that around the next bend a town or village will lie,
But after hours of walking, I'm back where I started, just the sand, the sea and I.

I have to face facts, I'm lost on a small island paradise,
In the middle of an ocean far, far away,
What do I do now, build a camp, light a fire, catch a fish,
All I have in my possession is a pen-knife and a pencil,
A map of Melbourne, a clean hanky and a pair of socks,
As I wander I find an old corked bottle left by the fleeing tide,
It looks like there's a message written deep inside.

The message reads, Dear Mary, Jack and Jane,
I'm writing this message,
In the hope it gets to you,
Daddy won't be home for a while,
So all help each other, take care,
My dreams are with you ever
My thoughts they leave you never,
Signed with love and kisses Harry Bellemy,
And dated fourth of May nineteen forty-three.

P J Littlefield

With You Soon

I feel you near me,
but yet you're far away from me
beyond the stars, as I lay upon white sand
I dream that you caress my hands
for our love knows no bounds
and I can not be stopped by hounds.
I feel the heat upon my brow,
and wonder if you remember how
I loved you so in such a way,
that not even the ocean could keep me away.
I hunger for your loving arms
and pray to hear your sexy charms.

Instead I am all alone
on this island praying to go home.
I hope they come to rescue me,
as life alone is not heavenly.
I've seen the footprints within the sand
walking to another land.
Is this where you lie at night,
because if it is then I shall write
to you each night, paper, thought or in the sand
I know you will be there holding my hand.
As I drift into your world,
I think about our baby girl.
She resembled you in such a way
I wish she was here today.
Instead I see bright lights,
then your handsome face, it feels so right.
I am with you now and so I see
that life without a family
is not one I wish to have
so shall we go and see my dad?

As he is here among the clouds
and I never say goodbye so now,
I leave this in your thoughts and hope,
that it reaches your port and/or your boat.

Alice Disu

Transition

The year smiles at sweet springtime's ways -
And passes on!
She dozes through long summer days -
And passes on!
Growing weary of autumn sweet
She trudges off on aching feet,
The wiles of winter's winds to meet -
And passes on!

She sees buds green upon the tree -
And passes on!
Then blossoms blown and falling free -
And passes on!
Before onset of winter's reign,
Bending brambles beneath the strain,
The year shares autumn's gifts again -
And passes on!

The best life offers comes with change -
And passes on!
The commonplace evolves from strange -
And passes on!
The heart outgrows all joy and grief,
And life's abidings are but brief;
New truth replaces old belief -
And passes on!

Dan Pugh

SOS

It's hot here, never thought I would complain
Not after my vitriol attacks on British rain
But oh, fresh water sounds
Like manna from heaven
And I long for fresh bread, fruit and chips

It's crazy I know but
Despite this salty embrace of the sea
I'm dying for *chips.*

Oh my unprotected head,
Am I going off the rails?
My hat is gone, don't know where
There must be other life here then.

Listen my love, if we never meet again,
Walk the dog won't you?
I miss his soft head - and yours,
Don't forget a little water, pure of course,
For the plants
Oh, my tongue feels like it's turned wooden.

Darling, there's a poem, desk drawer, top right,
Been meaning to send it off -
To that competition, remember?
My paintings you can sell
Doubt if you'll get rich on them
But who knows!

Well, I'm almost out of fuel so
I must go and find some moisture
Roots, leaves - *anything*
Love forever, your nomad.

Tracey Marshall

MESSAGE IN A BOTTLE

Friend,
I am David,
I wither in solitude.
On an island at sea.
I do not know this island.
But there's a mountain.
A mountain with two peaks
I shall be there.
I shall look for you,
For my eyes will never wander from where the sea meets the sky.
I shall light my fire and you shall see my sign.
Friend.
Do not discard me and cast me back into the seven seas as
You would a fish not fit to eat, for my very life is within this bottle.
I am a man, like you.
Is it too much to ask that I should not live like a man again?
Friend.
Come for me, and I will owe you my life.
Your name will become a legend, for I, David, will praise and speak
of you to every single person that I meet until the day I die.
Friend.
Don't discard me.
For I have become the genie in the lamp.
Release me and you shall be rewarded forever.

David.

T K Kennedy

Message In A Bottle

This message in a bottle is for you
If you are out there and should find it
Thrown up on the foreshore with the
Other bits and pieces. Debris of a life
That is no more. Lost when I was
Shipwrecked here

Left to brood about my fate, and yearn
For what I can not have. Not like Ben Gunn
For cheese. But for the smell of pavements
After rain, noises from the pub and the feel
Of children's arms around my neck.
These are the things I miss.

Yet this island can be beautiful, especially
At sunrise, when the sea sparkles and shifts
Like quicksilver, dancing in front of my eyes.
And again at sunset, when the treetops glow
Golden. Warming me inside and out.
Helping me get through the night

So think of me when at last you find my bottle
Think of me walking over empty sands, swimming in
Empty seas, dreaming of how I will get back
Sometime to the life that is more truly
Meant for me. Full of more familiar sounds
And full of people.

Fran Rawlings

FIRST GLASS MAIL

To whom it may concern
There are things I'd like to learn
Like was I the only lager lout?
And the only one to be pushed out?
I said the stewardess was cute
And would she share her parachute
My thoughts were clean and oh so pure
But I won't go on another package tour
My way of living might seem crude
But I'm running short of wholesome food
No knives or forks or cups or plates
The palm trees have only sell-by-dates
What else do I need, well may you ask
Some nice hot tea from a thermos flask
I've lived for months on lobster and crab
And all I want is a doner kebab
I had loads of food the other day
It was only a mirage and it faded away
I remembered as it slid into the sand
It was for the party that I'd planned

Stanley Swann

SOS

I've collected some shells, and tidied the beach,
Tried unsuccessfully to fish, my home-made net wouldn't reach,

I've had a good swim, and sunbathed for hours,
I've concocted a canopy of leaves, to shelter from the sun's powers,

I've talked to a turtle that visited me,
I've eaten some very funny things, but I'm longing for tea,

I'm missing my friends and family too,
Please rescue me *now* this kind of life just will not do!

June Ann Prescott

MESSAGE CALL

I hope this message will be found
When the sea decides to rest it on the ground
On this idyllic island where I feel no fear
No loneliness is an island
True contentment is here
From your distant friend (the beachcomber).

Emma Humphrey

BEARER

I'm all rolled up in here
Hoping someone'll lift me out
I'm a message in a bottle
Just in case there's any doubt

Here I'm suffocating
Awaiting my eager release
Won't someone hurry up and find me
- My bottle - oh do hurry please

My message is heavy
Anticipating hearing
My message is burden for me
But for you it is endearing

My message is gen'ral
May bring gladness or bring tear
But still worthy of a glance it is
Hoping to ring out loud and clear

I'm sure you'll feel privileged
If you be the finder
It will mean you're honoured owner
And may keep me in your binder

I hate this floating around
On the seas 'neath the ships' crews
I don't like it, nonetheless, I'm
Glad to be bearer of such news.

Barbara Sherlow

A MESSAGE IN A BOTTLE

I'm not alone,
for the love we share
engraves my heart,
I feel you here.

Though miles apart,
you fill my sky.
I feel as free
as seabirds fly.

Special memories
we hold dear,
join our minds,
keep us near.

I feel your breath
brush by the trees.
I taste your kiss
upon the breeze.

I close my eyes,
I see you smile.
I long your touch
and know that while,

We see the same
starlit night,
this love will always
shine as bright.

I hear your voice
in crashing waves.
With each new tide
I keep you safe.

Within my soul
until one day,
we'll meet again
I wait and pray.

Louise Ashley

MESSAGE IN A BOTTLE

I can't believe that I am here
Swept by the hurricane of time
On this island, so alone
Before the shipwreck, I was fine.

Unlike Dorothy in the 'Wizard of Oz',
There is no one here to befriend me,
No mythical characters or otherwise
Only the whispering of the trees.

I've survived on berries and coconut
Fish daily in the sea,
Collect kindling for a night-time fire,
I could murder a cup of tea.

My hair is dry and sun-bleached,
I'm skinny, but quite nicely tanned
I think my mind is playing tricks
Quite sure I can hear a band.

Oh please someone find my message
Nearly at the end of my tether,
I dream of being rescued one day
This island, will remember for ever.

You may wonder how I came by a bottle
It's no secret anymore,
It was either washed in by the sea
Or someone's been here before.

Joyce White

X Marks The Spot

I write this note, which may be my swan song,
Hoping it might be read before too long.
I'm stranded alone on this deserted isle
With nothing to see but sea - mile after mile.
I'm trusting this bottle will flow with the tide
To a popular resort - a well-known seaside.
Then maybe there'll be a inquisitive boy
Who will treat this bottle as a new toy.
He'll open it up to see what it says
And maybe - just maybe - before too many days,
My plight will be known and rescue made
And the worst of my nightmares will gradually fade.
Please God guide this bottle to a suitable place,
And I'll give to Thee endless thanks and praise.

Jean C Pease

MESSAGE IN A BOTTLE

Should this note be found
  Upon some pebbled shore
Please let my family know
  I won't be home no more
By the time they get this message
  I'll be dead and gone
I suppose, I was that fateful day
  When everything went wrong
The sea was really against us
  The winds just would not stop
It picked the ship into the air
  Then left it alone, to drop
The crew swam to safety
  To an island of sand and sun
And for a little while
  It was fine for everyone
But then the rations dwindled
  Few more days, then they were gone
People started dying, now I'm the only one
  Starving and all alone
Wishing our ship had stayed afloat
  Now it's the end, I think of family
And send all my love in this note.

Colleen Knight

HELP

I dreamt of a desert island where I could live on my own
Now in reality, shipwrecked, I'm on one, all alone
No food, no shelter from the heat
The sand's so hot it burns my feet

I can't swim to catch some fish
My stomach growls for food, I wish
I miss my family, I'm all alone
If only this island had a phone

I never dreamt it would be this way
No way on earth, do I want to stay
I write this message as my last plea
If you find this bottle, please come for me
My home is the place I want to be
To sit in my kitchen, with a nice cup of tea.

Patricia A M Lawson

THE CASTAWAYS' BOTTLE

Greetings this hungry day!
How will I chase this heat away?
Will I write this paper still?
With heavy hand and leaden quill.
This postage bottle corked and sent,
The ocean's mailbox, postage lent,
How could I have supposed
Inclusive by hand, the note enclosed
Full steam ahead the corals screech
Like fantastic seabirds before the beach
Will my heavy hand cease to tire
Before I can light - the beacon fire
By friction, moss and kindle sought
A borrowed memory, by children brought
Like marooned in books and legends still
Grinding away in our memory's mill
Like bread as wine sating hunger and thirst
These selfish thoughts not last but first -
One day my friend, we both shall see
How precious life can really be
Lost a thousand miles the tillers sway
Clung to, and kept, not given away
If I am not swallowed by sea or sand
Then upon some jetty proudly stand
Saved perhaps by a mariner's Dorey
From a saviour's captain? Another story!

G Jackson

SHIPWRECKED

I'm sitting on an island
Somewhere out at sea.
I think I've just been shipwrecked
But please don't pity me.

No more weekly washing,
No more household chores.
No more bills and taxes,
Or fighting other people's wars.

I'll laze about and think I'm Jane,
Make dresses out of leaves.
In my imagination, I'll see Tarzan,
Swinging in the trees.

Whoever finds this bottle
With my message in it.
Tell the folks back home,
I'm loving every minute.

Now my bottle's posted,
I feel a little sad.
If I see a passing ship,
I'll wave and shout like mad.

Now upon reflection,
Homeward bound I'd rather be.
Sitting, chatting, having fun,
With friends and family.

Peggy Howe

THE VIEW

With a lot behind and a bit in front
I've reached a time when looking back
Is hard because more has been done.
I've seen some changes to the world
And noticed as I pass along
That as it whirled I'm still just one.

I've viewed the rich, I've seen the poor
The hours and days and months and weeks
Add up to years, I've sewn my thread.
The garments that I made were worn
But changing trends turned each to rags
As each man born has ended dead.

J E Blissett

Tears

As my tears fall to the dust,
I know they must.
Pain will be as never before, blood
marks the earth's crust.
Father take the pain! Lift it off,
you know the just.
Let the troubles roll away as needs
around crumble to dust.
Floods oh! floods they flow, as the
pain increases, I trust.
Don't leave me now, don't turn
away, I feel so lost.
All now are asleep await the time
to meet the cost.

J H Mann

ALL ALONE

I assure you I am alone!
Far from help
I see the palms wave
And sunsets rare and a few ships gone
Man was once here
As an old bottle I have found
And on my person some note paper
I salvaged, still kept when
I thought hope was there
And it was not possible
To be quite alone on a once
Dream island now to nightmares too prone.
It is not possible to survive
Too long. Man is not civilised
As he would wish and self-
Sufficiency is short term
As with his thoughts, if with
Much time to contemplate.
He has lost the great gifts
That once made him not loose
Touch with things important.
Now self-important only to a dangerous world.
Beauty I do see here and if not swept away
I crave you remember my plight with all else not quite out of sight.

John Amsden

Sydney Darling - Billie Dear

(Dedicated to my beautiful nieces - Billie and Sydney. May we have the time to spend and the wisdom to make the most of it.)

Sydney darling - Billie dear,
Smell the roses, keep them near.
Always know that they're around
And if you look, they can be found.
Don't pass them by in daily life,
Too busy burdened down with strife;
Take time to search amongst the gloom,
Then when you find one - watch it bloom.

Oh Sydney darling - Billie dear,
Hear the angels, soft and clear.
Let choirs of heavenly sounding voices,
Guide you as you face life's choices.
Take time to learn the words they sing
And find the answers that they bring;
Then join the angels, sing along,
So others may just hear the song.

And Sydney darling - Billie dear,
Taste your freedom not its fear.
Explore life's beauty, free your mind;
Then pass on all the good you find.
Give thanks for that which comes your way
And give to those with less each day;
In thought and deed forever kind
Then one day Eden we shall find.

For all of this I've shared with you,
In thought and touch and word - so true;
So all that's left to whisper near,
Sydney darling - Billie dear:
Is love your sister, wipe her tear!
My Sydney darling - my Billie dear.

Ian Deal

Wish

It might be Tuesday,
It's got that hard edge to it,
I know it's a long time 'til the weekend,
Whatever that is.
I've seen people run across the sea
Hurrying to talk with someone
But they never stop to chat to me.

Sand's sharp today!

I've been alone before
Now I'm lonely.
Why, if I can dream food, can't I eat?
Why are they talking about me?
Why are you talking about me?
Why am I writing this to you?

Wish you were here
Instead of me.

Gareth Wyn Davies

DISTRESSED BY THE NEWS

As I walk into the sea
I ask 'Will you get this message from me?'
A scrap of paper, a pencil I had
Don't worry about me, my life's not bad.

Oh yes, I'm miles from the nearest town
But I never see a glowering frown.
Of yes, I have no roof at night
But I see the stars and the beauty of light.

My dearest wish I tell you now
Don't send a rescue please do vow.
I will make the best of what I've got
Even though the sun is hot.

The food I need I will find
So far I have well and truly dined.
No one here does me impair
Where am I? Yes, I am there.

Denise S Shaw

Message In A Bottle

I hope someone will find this
This is my silent plea
I hope someone will find this
And come and rescue me

I know you are a stranger
And I know I ask a lot
But you are my only hope for freedom
You are all that I have got

Strangers are simply friends
That we have yet to meet
So I'm asking you to be my friend
And make my life complete

Janet Larkin

UNTITLED

(Ps 36:8-9 'And you give the drink from the river of your pleasures for with you is the fountain of life')

From the crystal fountain
living water flows
cool and clean and healing
refreshing as it goes

Stand underneath the fountain
just stay there and receive
be touched by God's own spirit
the miracle is sealed

Ann Langley

A Message In A Bottle

I'm here on this island all alone
Goodness knows how far from home
Didn't even bring a phone
'Silly woman' I hear you say
'Can't even let her out for a day'

Oh yes I have the sea and sand
Maybe the decor's very grand
Palm trees wafting in the breeze
How I wish I was one of these
Then pangs of hunger wouldn't strike

Do you know just what I'd like?
Chocolate bars piled up high
Blowing my diet plans sky high
I wished I'd brought my old straw hat
But now there's not much chance of that

'Everything has to stay on board'
The captain roared. Oh my Lord, no clothes
No money, nothing left
Swim for our lives, soon bereft

Everyone else just disappeared
Eaten by sharks is what I feared
So if you find this bottle at all
Give my love to one and all
Suddenly from behind a tree
A tall, well tanned and handsome hunk
It's George Clooney carrying a trunk

Already I'm feeling ten years younger
So kids I'm staying a little bit longer
Don't hurry with that rescue boat
When I come home I'll make you gloat

Carole Hanson

A MESSAGE IN A BOTTLE

As I stand on this sand, on this little island,
I don't feel my outlook's terrific.
Cast away one sad day on this deserted cay,
Lost somewhere amid the Pacific.

Looking round all I've found, lying here on the ground,
Is a bottle that used to hold rum.
This bottle I've got'll be useful or not'll
Depending whether it can overcome.

If it braves all the waves, and fortune behaves,
Maybe it will reach some far shore.
Where mayhap some smart chap, with a good thinking cap
Will soon make two plus two equal four.

Find the note that I wrote and charter a boat,
And so rescue this maid in distress.
How I pray for the day that his boat comes my way,
But there's one thing I have to confess.

Now my yen is for men, when I see one again
After living here left on the shelf,
I may say, 'Let's just stay on this beautiful cay.
And the world can look after itself!'

J D Goodspeed

MESSAGE IN A BOTTLE

I found a bottle in the sand
Discarded by the sea
A message in it wrote by hand
Found by little me.
Who was this message meant for
What on earth did it all mean
It was such a lovely rapport
It was just like a dream
I'm the lucky maiden the bottle I found
But here I am, I'm all alone
The writer of this message is not around
So I'll take the message home.

Dawn Moore

A Cay Day

All alone, no interaction,
Nothing to do, no satisfaction.
Frightened and distressed,
Secluded and depressed.
No welcome smile, and no pertinacious throng,
A constant yearning to belong.
I long to be homeward bound, from a lesser day,
If anyone found my bottle, all my troubles will be 'cast away'.

John P Evans

Rescue Me

I had to get away
To let us have our space
But now I am stranded here
And may never get to say
That I really do love you
That I wasn't always right
That you were the only one for me
And as I think of you this night
I am filled with dread and fear
That I may never see your face again
Or hear your voice
And it hurts inside like real pain
So I am writing you a message in a bottle
So one day you can rescue me
Like you did so many years ago
And we could perhaps be happy again . . .

Lindsey Brown

A Message In A Bottle

I found a message in a bottle
Washed up on the shore
It read oh please help me
You see I went out for a paddle
And the tide came sweeping in
I realised I was stranded
You see I just can't swim
I'm stuck here on this island
And I'm out here all alone
I'm tired and cold and hungry
I just want to get back home
If anybody finds this
Message that I send
And tries their best to save me
They will be my special friend.

Gillian Morrisey

THE SORCERER

I am in little shock.
Not troubled by thought or look,
I stand here the tyrant of a rock
And do not move to meet my council.

Great am I in limiting.
I cannot but tie myself
With a soothsayer look.

Nicola Barnes

SECLUSION AMIDST

SOS, SOS, have you got this SOS?
Help me quick, I'm in a mess
Caught adrift on troubled seas
Read my plight and hear my pleas

On this island cold and bleak
Hope and solace do I seek
Send a ship to rescue me
'Fore I reach insanity

Sing a shanty, sing a dirge
'Captain Bligh became my scourge'
Mutinous unto the end
Bottled bounty do I send

Answer quick, answer pray
Come, that we might sail away
On this island life is dead
Loneliness absorbs my head

Water, water everywhere
None to drink I do declare
People, people all around
All a'speaking make no sound

On this island millions dwell
Make my life a living hell
All their trifling, turgid talk
Fills the cracks of life like caulk

Reason not with common sense
Never known intelligence
Save me from this mindless grave
Reach me on the strongest wave

Cherry

MESSAGE IN A BOTTLE

Please do find me, I am so alone,
There's nothing I can do,
So I've sent a message in a bottle,
Trusting it will float to you.

No food or drink, I'm desperate,
I don't need to slim this way,
Everywhere is oh! so desolate
No one with whom to play.

Surely you are missing me,
Now prove to me you care,
Everything I will forget,
Everything I will share.

I have very little here to give,
But if you rescue me
You can take me as I am
Now what fun that would be.

Feeling destitute, forsaken,
I said my prayers, have faith,
Perhaps if I sleep, I shall awaken
To see a miracle taken place.

So message in a bottle,
Set sail, listen to my plea,
Whoever takes the stopper out,
Please come and collect me.

D Wilbraham

FOR KATHLEEN AND LILIAN

A message in a bottle
To my sisters I do send,
With the hope that they will find it,
And an ear that they will lend.

I've loved you dearly, both of you,
Through good times, and the bad,
And I want to thank the both of you
For support that I have had.

Through many operations,
Bereavements, grief and all,
You've been there for me, both of you,
And I've come through, walking tall;.

We've also had some happy times
The three of us, to share,
Even tho' we're far apart
And somewhat, the worse for wear.

We're almost in our dotage, but
We still have fun to share,
Whenever we make the journey
From north and south, to 'there'.

One comes down from Scotland,
The other, up from Kent,
We all meet in the middle
For our annual event.

I'd like to thank the both of you,
Tell you 'I love you' too,
The world would be a better place
For more folk 'the like' of you.

Barbara Whitworth

HOMESICKNESS

I have a wish to be at home in spring,
far from the lonely ocean's cry,
among the forest's dappled light
where rainbow shades of birds in flight
brush the air as they go winging by.

I long to smell the scent of summer rose
filing the dawning flush of newborn day,
see butterflies with wings aglow
hovering where blossomed borders grow,
in an English garden, far away.

I yearn to roam in autumn's tranquil peace
under a canopy of russet leaves,
see the knee-deep corn of ripened gold
trace the river's course, the hillside fold,
the sunlight golden on the waiting sheaves.

Shall I again see winter's fields and lakes,
among the countryside I loved to roam,
and will I ever sit alone with you
talking of things we used to do,
in the comfort of our love - back again at home.

Ann Rutherford

Love Life

I won't waste precious paper, the boat sank, I swam, I'm here.
Tell my family my last thoughts were of their future. Don't sit
around maudlin - it's all part of life's tapestry - we all die -
this is my time.
I don't go willingly - I will watch the horizon daily - but being
sensible - no one is expected.
I have gloried in my life to the sunrise, the beauty of new days,
the wonder of the seasons, the comfort of the night, the stars in
the heavens. No home or garden or person can ever match the
feelings it brings, ever could.
I hope I never disappointed you all. I gave all I had in time,
energy, love and trust and would do it all again -
wholeheartedly. Every one of you are in my heart - always,
eternally. My thoughts of you will soar with my soul and be part
of your future - somewhere my love will surround you - in joy.
My message is 'love life, let it embrace you, my faint pattern is
there in your new future'.

Jean Horsham

Please Rescue Me

If you should find this bottle
Floating on the sea,
Please look inside and read my note
Then come and rescue me.

I'm trapped here on this island
Due south of Hotland Bay,
My boat is wrecked, I hit a rock
And I can't get away.

Oh this overpowering heat
No shelter from the sun,
I sailed out here to get a tan,
Not to melt and burn.

There is no sign of man or beast
I've gathered a few nuts to eat,
I'd love a bowl of Shredded Wheat
And a nice cup of tea.

Tomorrow I'll wash all my clothes in the sea,
Hang them out to dry
And then I'll wash me.
If at that time you should chance to come by,
Just whistle three times
'Cause believe me I'm shy.

I've never been so lonely, hungry and afraid,
So many creepy crawlies with lots of legs and wings,
On bended knees I'm begging you,
Take me back to human beings.

Joan Lawson

Some Message!

Hello! Hello! You have unscrewed my top,
Please read the lines inside, no compass have I got,
I just bob with wind and tide, nor
Can I tell the time, just light and dark I know,
A blinding sparkle day, shimmering black the night,
I bobbed like this before when,
Flung from ship to shore, lost,
Alone upon the sand, pecked, knocked about,
Strutting birds, seeking bills, would
I be cracked across the back, broken neck,
Disintegrated, ground to grains of sand?
When I felt a seeking hand, not
Flung back to the ocean, but getting stroked, felt,
A whispering voice I heard,
'Thank God I have found a bottle
What can I find to scratch a message,
Catch a passing sailor's eye,
A sunny sparkle in the water,
Something to identify this island, someone
Stuck upon it, survivor of a storm?'
So here I am full of torn leaves,
Hope someone will suss out the letters,
Put this island's name together,
Rescue the rescuer who rescued me,
Jesus' love, our lifeboat to the mainland.

Anne Mary McMullan

IN THE BEGINNING WAS THE WORD

The poet of old 'shot his arrow into the air;
it fell to earth he knew not where' -
so if I 'throw my bottle into the sea'
a comparison maybe drawn -
for I know not where my message will land.
(Picked up or lost and forlorn!)
Nevertheless I'm tossing it in,
trusting that others for Him I'll win!

Patricia Lawrence

Do Me A Favour

Tell the wife I'm fine.
Boy, these hula-girls are so friendly.
I may be getting hay-fever.
The Chief says I'm still 'No 1 fella' -
I watch my back, just in case.
I find sucking-pig filling - but greasy.
Haven't caught one myself yet.
They're building me a new cabin.
I can't get 'em to understand about windows -
And me a double glazing salesman.
Our volcano is pretty quiet these days.
I play along with the 'Fire-God Him Angry' set.
I spend ages with the mums and kids, making them laugh.
Amazing, how much of the local brew is offered.
We found a baby whale last week.
Got it out to sea and the mother nearly swamped us.
I've made a fast one-man canoe -
Paddles and a decent seat will follow.
Tell her I'm held captive.
Tell her I'm head-warrior, Mr Nasty.
Tell her what you like.
I'm not leaving this little number.

Brian Phillips

Au Revoir

You, my love, are gone, no more your dear
familiar face to see; and yet, though parted, still you live on
in hearts touched by your love and care,
lives that have been transformed, that with yours have had a share.

A beloved friend of many passing years,
yet these eyes which now spill with tears
at your passing will, with healing time
look inwards to the memories that are forever mine.

So for now, my love, goodnight,
another day we'll meet in heavenly light;
where pain and partings are no more,
and love, our love, shared upon this earth, shall be for evermore.

Catherine Riley

A Castaway

A castaway maybe
But I'm happy being me
Though my thoughts on you will roam
I'm in no hurry to go home.

My survival kit is simple,
Water, fish and prayer,
And a chance to study issues,
That some had to give up in despair.

Jill Ives

MESSAGE IN A BOTTLE

I have been on this island many days,
with its mountain of great elevation
my only companion is an angel he says,
what he told me was quite a revelation.

He told me this island is called Patmos,
though this was a revelation to me,
as to who is Pat Moss, I'm at a loss,
to me it's a big rock in the sea!

He told me some stories that opened my eye,
of things to come in the end days,
I sincerely hope that they come after I die,
if there is half a truth in what he says!

With horsemen and plagues running free,
and many headed monsters that throttle,
and angels and armies and beasts of the sea,
please rescue me if you find this bottle!

John The Beloved

Just To Let You Know

There was once a jolly sailor boy who wandered off to sea
With a jaunty gait and his duffel bag, a sprightly lad was he
Away he went on a sunny day on an ocean as smooth as silk
When out of the blue a terrible storm, pressing clouds
even blacker than ink!

The poor little ship was battered and torn when struck by a
monstrous wave
'Each man for himself' was the captain's cry - a command to
his matelot's brave
Our staunch jolly tar battled long in the brine, as the cruel
storm ranted and raged
When a raft sweeping by was his one final chance, his life
by a miracle saved.

Ahead he espied a carpet of gold, a welcoming sight for his eyes
A fringe of palms, a sun-kissed beach - his gateway to paradise
He found for himself a sheltering cave, a haven to keep him from harm
Woven branches and reeds were his table and chair, and a bed
that was cosy and warm.

He feasted each day on berries and fruit, with a special fine treat
for his tea
Milk from a coconut tasty and sweet, and succulent fish from the sea
A life free and easy with never a care, oh surely this must be his fate
For he met on the shore a shy dusky maid, who consented to
be his sweet mate.

One day as he walked on the shimmering sand, a bottle of green
he espied
So he sent out a message maybe someone would find, and threw
it way into the tide
'I happily live on a paradise isle, and must say there's nothing I lack
You are welcomed to join me if you feel so inclined, for I'm
certainly not coming back!

Barbara Davies

SOS . . .

I used to be the owner of
  A full and happy heart;
Never one to dump a man
  And to the next one dart.
I'm lonely, lost and vulnerable.
  In need of honest love,
One that flows with constant ease,
  Just like the clouds above.
I *need* to trust! I *need* to share!
  For now and from here on . . .
Anything is better than
  A can of soup for one.
Hey Mr! I won't let you down;
  It's not my style you see,
I could never do to you
  What someone did to me.
Any man will do for me
  So long as he is kind,
Who doesn't leave me at the hands
  Of demons in my mind.
This message to your shore I send,
  Please read me loud and clear . . .
I'll sign off now . . . be kind . . . bye . . . ciao . . .

(From Nin in Lancashire)

Linda Zulaica

A Yachtsman's Plea

Will I ever see you all again, my family and my home?
Frenziedly I search the brain in my sorely addled dome.
The relentless sun has rendered me a scorched and sorry wreck
I throw this bottle in the sea, my last hope to save my neck!
My wildest dreams at dead of night of food and drink are filled
Superbly served to my delight with champagne ready chilled!
I know I've wandered far and wide neglecting those I love,
My lesson's learned, I'll sink my pride if I get the chance to prove
How much you really mean to me you dear ones waiting there
No more will I go out to sea, your lives are mine to share.
I'll be a husband, father, son . . . remain in my domicile
And really know the race is run if I'm rescued from this isle.

Eileen Martin

QUESTIONING LIFE

Life is a mystery in itself,
Who has all the answers?
Each day I ask myself,
What exactly is the meaning of life?
We are born waiting to die,
What's the point? I constantly wonder why.
Is there a purpose we must achieve?
Does God have the answers up his sleeves?
Where do we go from here?
Is there such places as heaven and hell?
Questions, questions, I ask myself,
Life is a mystery in itself,
Who has all the answers?

Ruthie Gardner-Sonderegger

To Steve

I can only say on paper,
What I would like to say in voice,
But I can't express in sound,
So I only have one choice,
To write the way I feel,
To pen I love you so
To say in black and white
All the things that you should know
Like the closeness of a pen,
On the paper that I write,
That's how close that I will be,
Every day and every night,
But unlike the ink within,
That runs out into thin air,
I'll always be around,
To show how much I care.

Linda Wade

BOTTLE BUOY

Message in a bottle all my tears are shed
I knew one day the time would come
I never could turn down a challenge
Always ready for a dare
So - bottle buoy

How soon we learned to disregard
The whirring noise above
How you daily watched our movements
I wonder what went round your head
He must have been so worried
Bottle buoy

Now it's time to face the music,
Armed with every daily thought,
Part of the deal all signed and sealed.
So bottle buoy you go first
I won't be far behind
When they land they will find me
As you left me full of joy
Missing my buoy.

Sevtlana Edwards

ME-THUSELUM!

This is my history since dinner, I must admit:
All I know is that I slide against glass;
That I can't reach the cork to push it.
I'm tossed about on this tidal spume
In cold molten sand, I'm sensing doom.

Stuck as I am, in this tube, transparent
Cell, to stare through at waves raging near rocks
Hoping some stray Lorelei will present
This slave in a bottle to a sailor:
If he gives me freedom, I'll wash his sea-socks!

Suzanne Stratful

All Washed Up

I've always been big and wanted to diet,
But this is so drastic I don't want to try it.

Because here am I stranded with no food and water
Just like a poor lamb being led to the slaughter.

The idea of cruising seemed fun and terrific
So how come I'm shipwrecked out in the Pacific?

This island's deserted, I've no one to talk to
It's so bloomin' tiny there's nowhere to walk to.

The sun's blazing down and I've no factor seven
Oh how I would love to be back home in Devon.

But I do have this bottle, a pencil and paper
So I'll give it a try cos I'm sick of this caper.

My message is written and thrown in the foam
If you happen to find it I'd love to go home.

If you'd come and fetch me I'd really be grateful
By the way, I love roast spuds, so bring me a plateful!

Jessica Sykes

Sense And Sensuality

Dionysus - you god of cup and revelry
And other satisfying kinds of devilry
The sensuality of belly dancers
The husky voice of willing lovers' answers
And self-indulgence when we deem to sin
Smooth shapeliness that is a violin.
The hit between the shoulder-blade that grabs
When foot down on hot rod's gas pedal stabs.
The dipping swooping roller coaster ride,
The wiggle of a tight-jeaned girl's backside
Warm rapture from a glass of vintage wine
Table of superb cuisine when we dine.
Oh, I could enthuse on for evermore.
Just what else is human perception for?
And so that I can carry on the style
Just rescue me from this forsaken isle.

Derrick Mitchell

My Silent Island

Long since have passed the raging storms,
That abandoned me on this virgin land.
It is days, weeks, months or maybe -
A year . . . I wonder . . . I wonder.
A prisoner of my own destiny.
Yet . . . I reign as a king in my own dominion,
But an exile of my own misfortune,
A captive of my own keeping.
Oh how I miss the sound and touch of another human soul.
From the elation of joy to the sorrow of tears,
And the voices of children in song with all their purity and innocence.
I long for the warmth of words
The warmth of wisdom
The warmth of the body
But most of all the warmth of love,
Nature seems to have claimed me
Although never immune . . . I am under her influence,
I have sheltered from her rains
Been warmed by her sun
Quenched my thirst with her water
And picked the fruits of her harvest
For without her I would not be here.

In the year 2000 somewhere in the pacific ocean,
To the finder of this bottle, please inform Eleanor
Trapnell, I love her dearly.

Derrick James Hardy

MEMO TO THE PRIME MINISTER

(A villanelle)

I voted for you, Tony Blair,
I was so glad New Labour won;
The future seemed to be set fair.

It was a night beyond compare -
The losing Tories on the run;
I voted for you, Tony Blair.

There was a feeling in the air
Of dreams come true for everyone;
The future seemed to be set fair.

The policies you brought to bear
Were second, it appeared, to none;
I voted for you, Tony Blair.

But years have passed and I'm aware
That very much remains undone:
The future seemed to be set fair.

Yet still, PM, your hopes I share;
Life for us all should be more fun.
I voted for you, Tony Blair,
The future seemed to be set fair.

Sheila Burnett

From The Shore Of Isolation

I was like any other man
Who seeks to command the waves of life,
But I was not steady at the helm
When the currents changed and squalls were rife.

My hands were not firm upon the wheel.
My world went down under heavy seas
Which set me aside on an unknown shore,
Alone with my sack of memories.

Now, set apart from my fellow-man,
I see that I needed to meet the storm:
I was unready to share my life,
Expecting all others to conform.

So I have drunk to the bitter dregs.
Myself, like a bottle, is clear as glass.
Curled in these words is my message to those
Out of whose lives I seemed to pass.

The man you knew has died on the rocks
Of ultimate challenge. This man is new.
Save me from loneliness. Let me prove
The self I am now is right and true.

Pamela Constantine

A MOTHER'S LAST WORDS

I've been in your world to help you,
I taught you the best I could,
I loved you all with all my heart,
As a proper mother should.

And on the day I left you,
I know you were filled with sorrow,
But please I beg you now,
Be happy for me that I don't face a painful tomorrow.

My road was growing weary,
And I was so tired too,
And when my maker called me,
I went to him and had to leave you.

I left you not forever,
But only for a while,
One day we'll be together,
Then I can see you smile.

I want you to know that I'm happy,
Here, there's no suffering or pain,
Just peace and lovely surroundings,
No illness to drive me insane.

So please be happy for me,
And after the first year has passed,
You'll realise what I mean by this,
And you'll all be happy at last.

Now I will finish my letter,
For one day I know you'll all come,
And we'll all be happy together,
And I'll choose my final time.

Joyce Jackson

No More! No More!

Hope my message darling reaches you very soon,
On this tiny desert island I've been marooned.
Because the huge ship bringing me home to you,
Hit a large rock and floundered under briny blue.
I the sole survivor, think I'm going crazy,
Events of that day have now turned very haze!
Coconuts often fall to the hot sandy floor,
But my aching stomach cries out, no more! No more!
Love could you send out a search party for me,
For I am scared and from this island must be freed.

S Mullinger

HELP!

I've had enough of coconuts
I've had enough of trees,
I'd like to get away from here
Oh listen to my pleas.
I don't know how I got here,
I don't know if I'm sane,
Please won't you send a boat,
A ship, a raft, an aeroplane.
I need to hear a human voice,
I need to know you're there,
So find this note and act upon
And show me that you care.

Ann Stringer

Rescue Me

I'm no Esther Williams or sexy Andress
Yet I'm wrecked on an island, I'm in a mess.
My skin is all scaly with salt from the sea
Won't someone take pity and please rescue me.

The mosquitoes all bite me, I'm covered in bumps,
My hair looks like seaweed, I'm down in the dumps.
The island is tiny, there is not much to pick,
The fish are all spiny, the fruit makes me sick.

My dress is all tattered, my nails badly torn,
I'm all over sunburn and feeling forlorn.
If nobody finds me I think I shall scream
Can I hear an alarm clock? Glory be, it's a dream.

L E Gill

Message In A Bottle

If you find this message
(But I doubt you ever will)
And think to come and rescue me
Please don't bring a pill.
I'm stranded on this island
I think it's name is Jade
It's rocky and it's sandy
So bring a pick and a spade.
It's all you'll need to bury me
For I am failing fast
And the message in this bottle
Will be my very last.
But if you should ignore it
To go off and have some fun
Don't worry, mate, you're doing
Just what I would have done.

Jean Trigg

To My Father

I love you, my father, and I always shall.
I hope that I'll see you again.
I think of your kindness and love every day.
You are the most caring of men.

I think of the lovely doll's house that you made,
It gave me such hours of play.
I think of my rubber dolls, Billy and Bob.
I played with them both every day.

At Christmas, my stocking was full to the top,
With toys peeping out from the rim
And fruit and nuts, chocolate and sweets in the toe,
I looked while the light was still dim.

At Easter an Easter egg always appeared
With chocolates inside tightly packed
And birthdays were joyful with presents galore.
You made sure that I never lacked.

And as I grew older your love and your care
Were lavished, whenever I came
For soothing advice or a comforting arm
Your wise counsel always the same.

My father I love you and I always shall
And if I don't see you again
I want you to know that I'd always choose you,
My dad, above all other men.

Joyce M Turner

A MESSAGE IN A BOTTLE

This is a wonderful island,
I'm waiting for someone to come
To bring me champagne and caviar
Whisky, brandy and rum.
I'll try and keep my patience
While waiting on the shore,
Don't forget a bottle opener
Who could ask for more?
We'll make a little love nest,
I'll order a full moon,
Stars and wafting breezes -
So someone, find me soon.

Win Forster

DESERT ISLAND

I was shipwrecked and
Marooned on this island
So blue
Only a piece of paper to
Write a message or two

What would I write, what
Could I say
Maybe there'll be a ship, that'll
Pass this way

I'm awash with millions
Of waves
Cascading towards me
Hoping I'll be saved

And as my footprints dance
Across the shore
And the waves wash in and
Out once more

And as the sun beats down
The sand is hot
A paradise island never
To be forgot.

Marilyn Davidson

MY SPECIAL ISLAND

If by chance you find my bottle
I love living here and take many a toddle
But I fantasise all the time and my mind boggles
Please bring me a Cornish pasty to coddle.

Jean Jarrett

CASTAWAY

I've been castaway on this island
Since goodness only knows when
Maybe it's been a month, but it
Could even have been ten.
Time has lost all meaning,
I'm alone and very sad
I wish I had some company
Then I would not feel so bad
I live on nuts and berries
And certain kind of leaves
I found a mountain stream
That's like nectar to the bees.
Then one day I found a bottle
So someone's been here before
Now I'm going to send a message
To the two people that I adore.
I only hope it reaches them
So they will know I'm still alive
I'm going to do my very best
To be happy and survive:
I can picture when we meet again
What a reunion it will be
It will be worth my while in exile,
Or simply lost at sea.
The message I send is 'I love you both'
I always have and I always will
Say a prayer for me and I will
Soon be back, racing you down the hill
Now my bottle is on its way
May it reach some distant shore
May God grant my prayer and I will
Be home again with the loved ones I adore.

K G Ney

My Love

Now I am gone
Keep thy heart free
Just carry on
And you will see
The sun shining
Giving you courage
So keep smiling
On your way

Think of the happy hours
We had together
Which were all just 'ours'
You will feel better
One must enjoy life as it is
'Til time comes to go
It can be filled with 'bliss'
As memories flow

Look forward to a good day
No thought of sigh
Which will come your way
Seek a fresh life
In a spiritual manner
Your heart will feel lighter
As you carry your banner
Feeling we are together

Josephine Foreman

Desert Fun

If you ever find this message
'Oy' I need some grub
I am no good at fishing
I nearly ate a shrub
What about sausage and mash
A bowl of custard and jelly
'Oh' and a drop of brandy
To warm my belly
I talk to myself you know
Well I need some company
How about a kiss
'Oy' please come to me
I need a coffee right now
Don't forget the ginger nuts
I want you, now behave
Well I know some huts
Behave yourself young lady
There's plenty of time for that
Right now I need the loo
I can only find my hat
Is that a figure I see
In the distance over there
As long as it is you
Then boy I do not care
Wait a minute, am I seeing things
It must have been a mirage
No there it is me girl
On that floating barge
All of a sudden I can't believe it's true
My prayers have been answered, it's you.

C Moorhouse

Time's Up

With pencil stub on paper scrap
I now write about my mishap
Plunged upon a hostile beach
By contraption beyond tide's reach.

Having a pidgin caption
'Sailing much brings satisfaction'.
On my body rain beats a tune
Enforcing shelter by the dune.

A burst of sun then warms my clothes
Compelling me to nod and doze.
Dreams of a pretty girl in peach
Broken by blood-curdling screech.

A scraggy bird circles around.
With fear my heart begins to pound.
'Tis of an alien culture
Surely it must be a vulture.

A boat approaches at great speed
Piloted by a shouting Swede
'Your time expired hours ago
Now hurry back with pedalo.'

I dash across the muddy sand
Juggling my shoes in trembling hand
On the pedalo, breath shorter,
Aquaplane into the water.

Whilst they chase me at full throttle
Into the sea I drop the bottle.
Words preserved for posterity
Thanks to ambidexterity.

Dennis Walker

MONEY CAN'T BUY A BOAT

I always thought it would be romantic
To be among sands, sea and palm trees
But life like dreams is far removed from reality
I fell from a cruise ship showing off to mates
By the time they realised it was all too late
So I swam to this tiny island which isn't much
No girls, no drink and no fish and chip shops as such
I did try my hand at some fishing without success
I'm not a vegetarian and grass doesn't taste best
I did have a pencil and paper and one of my talents
You mocked about those poems I used to write
So I'm sending you one last one in this bottle
You begged me not to go on the trip, it looks now
As if you were right, women usually are
I should have taken you with me after I won the lottery
It was amazing how many friends I acquired
But as money is no use to me on a desert island
And to say goodbye to you is all that's required

Melanie M Burgess

FINAL FLING

Boom of the outer deep and lift of rolling waves
Has carried me to island solitude with bare horizon days.
Predictive sky, unyielding palms, scrubbed beach before a sultry cave;
Yet no Man Friday, hula girl or ocean roving strays.

I have scrawled a bottled message, hurled with sailor's swear
Beyond the reef toward the coral flash of setting sun
On sea that links me to another shore in prayer.
Chance pulls a face but I am not yet done.

Ever the optimist. A passing ship, a plane - who knows?
Perhaps my fret will bob to land in weeks not years,
Though profitless; this compass point unknown: whatever fate suppose.
A wry defiance in my toast, whoever reads it - 'Cheers!'

Adrian Cooper

INFORMATION

We hope you have enjoyed reading this book - and that you will continue to enjoy it in the coming years.

If you like reading and writing poetry drop us a line, or give us a call, and we'll send you a free information pack.

Write to :-